**W9-BIM-488**

-ig as in pig

Kelly Doudna

Consulting Editor Monica Marx, M.A./Reading Specialist

Published by SandCastle™, an imprint of ABDO Publishing Company, 4940 Viking Drive, Edina, Minnesota 55435.

Printed in the United States.

Credits
Edited by: Pam Price
Curriculum Coordinator: Nancy Tuminelly
Cover and Interior Design and Production: Mighty Media
Photo Credits: Corel, Kelly Doudna, Eyewire Images, Hemera, PhotoDisc, Stockbyte

Library of Congress Cataloging-in-Publication Data

Doudna, Kelly, 1963-
     -ig as in pig / Kelly Doudna ; consulting editor, Monica Marx.
        p. cm. -- (Word families. Set III)
     Summary: Introduces, in brief text and illustrations, the use of the letter combination "ig" in such words as "pig," "sprig," "fig," and "twig."
     ISBN 1-59197-236-1
     1. Readers (Primary) [1. Vocabulary. 2. Reading.] I. Marx, Monica. II. Title.

PE1119 .D675833 2003
428.1--dc21   2002037911

SandCastle™ books are created by a professional team of educators, reading specialists, and content developers around five essential components that include phonemic awareness, phonics, vocabulary, text comprehension, and fluency. All books are written, reviewed, and leveled for guided reading, early intervention reading, and Accelerated Reader® programs and designed for use in shared, guided, and independent reading and writing activities to support a balanced approach to literacy instruction.

Let Us Know

After reading the book, SandCastle would like you to tell us your stories about reading. What is your favorite page? Was there something hard that you needed help with? Share the ups and downs of learning to read. We want to hear from you! To get posted on the ABDO Publishing Company Web site, send us e-mail at:

sandcastle@abdopub.com

SandCastle Level: Beginning

-ig Words

dig

jig

pig

rig

twig

wig

Phil and Mitch like to
dig in the sand.

The leprechaun dances
a jig.

The pig is pink with a
black spot.

A big truck is also called a rig.

7

The black bird sits on a twig.

Trish wears a blue wig.

10

The Big Pig

This pig
is really big.
The big pig
likes to dig.

13

14

The big pig
finds a silly wig.

The pig
puts on the wig
and dances a jig.

17

The big pig
finds a sprig.

The sprig is on
the end of a twig.

19

The big pig
finds a rig.

The rig is big
enough for the pig,
the wig, and the twig.

The -ig Word Family

big	rig
dig	sprig
fig	swig
gig	twig
jig	wig
pig	

Glossary

Some of the words in this list may have more than one meaning. The meaning listed here reflects the way the word is used in the book.

jig　　　　a quick and lively dance

leprechaun an elf of Irish folklore

rig　　　　a large truck often used for hauling freight

sprig　　　a small twig or shoot

twig　　　a thin, small branch of a tree or shrub

wig　　　　real or artificial hair made to be worn on the head

About SandCastle™

A professional team of educators, reading specialists, and content developers created the SandCastle™ series to support young readers as they develop reading skills and strategies and increase their general knowledge. The SandCastle™ series has four levels that correspond to early literacy development in young children. The levels are provided to help teachers and parents select the appropriate books for young readers.

Emerging Readers
(no flags)

Beginning Readers
(1 flag)

Transitional Readers
(2 flags)

Fluent Readers
(3 flags)

These levels are meant only as a guide. All levels are subject to change.

To see a complete list of SandCastle™ books and other nonfiction titles from ABDO Publishing Company, visit www.abdopub.com or contact us at:

4940 Viking Drive, Edina, Minnesota 55435 • 1-800-800-1312 • fax: 1-952-831-1632